Ginger

Activity Book 3

EARLY START EDITION
CLASS 3

Cornelsen

Contents

Symbols

 listen to CD 1 • track 23

CD 1.23

 read

 speak

 write

Welcome aboard! My family photos

I 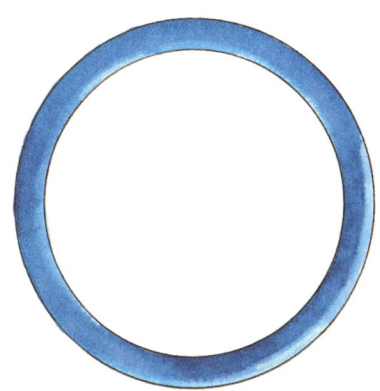 Glue or draw your family photos here. Write the words.

_____   _____

_____   _____

_____   _____

Seine Familie vorstellen (S. 55 f.)

Welcome aboard! School things

1 ○ **Count the school things. Write sentences.**

> books • pencils
> pencil cases • pens
> rubbers • schoolbags

There are _____ _____ _____

_____ _____

_____ _____

2 ○ **Write what you've got in your pencil case.**

I've got _____

_____

1 Complete the sentences.

2 Colour T-shirt number 6. Write about it.

blue
brown
green
orange
red
yellow

1 T-shirt number 1 is orange and __ _____

2 T-shirt number 2 is _____ _____

3 _____ _____

4 _____

5 _____ _____ __ _____

6 _____

Farbwörter schreiben (S. 61)

Welcome aboard! Telephone calls

1 🔘 Listen and number the people in the right order.
CD 1.23

2 Draw lines between the crew and their countries.
Complete the sentences.

Captain Storm is   Debbie _____   Ravi _____

from _____   _____   _____

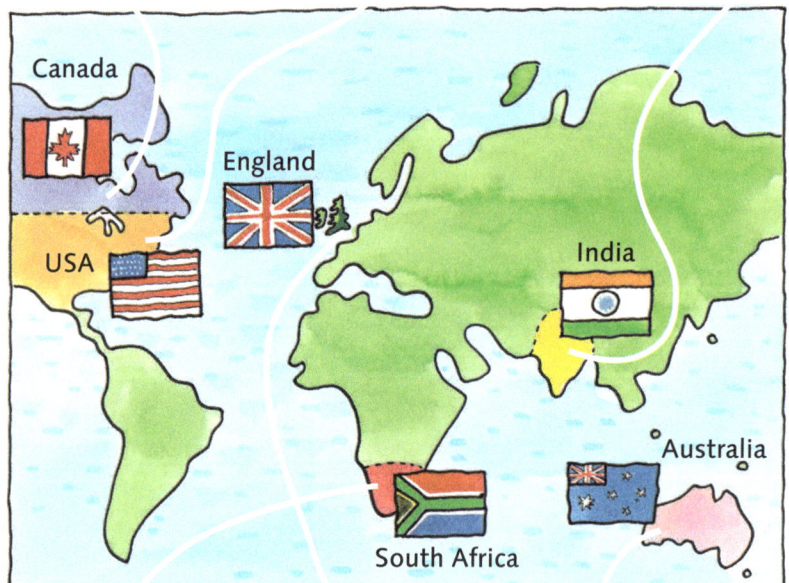

Canada
England
USA
India
Australia
South Africa

Dr Heal _____   Ginger _____   Colin _____

_____   ___ - _____   _____

Dialoge verstehen, Sätze vervollständigen (S. 63 f.)

Welcome aboard! Boarding card

1  Read Ginger's boarding card.

Name
Ginger

From
England

Hair
red

Eyes
blue

Deck
orange

Cabin
3

2 Fill in your boarding card. Cut out your boarding card.

Name

From

Hair

Eyes

Deck

Cabin

Eine Bordkarte lesen und ausfüllen (S. 64)

Welcome aboard!

Boarding
card

Breakfast tables

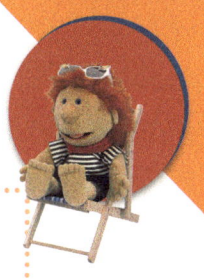

1 Talk about the tables.

2 What's missing on the breakfast tables? Write the words. Draw the things.

cornflakes • bread
egg • honey • milk
orange juice

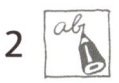

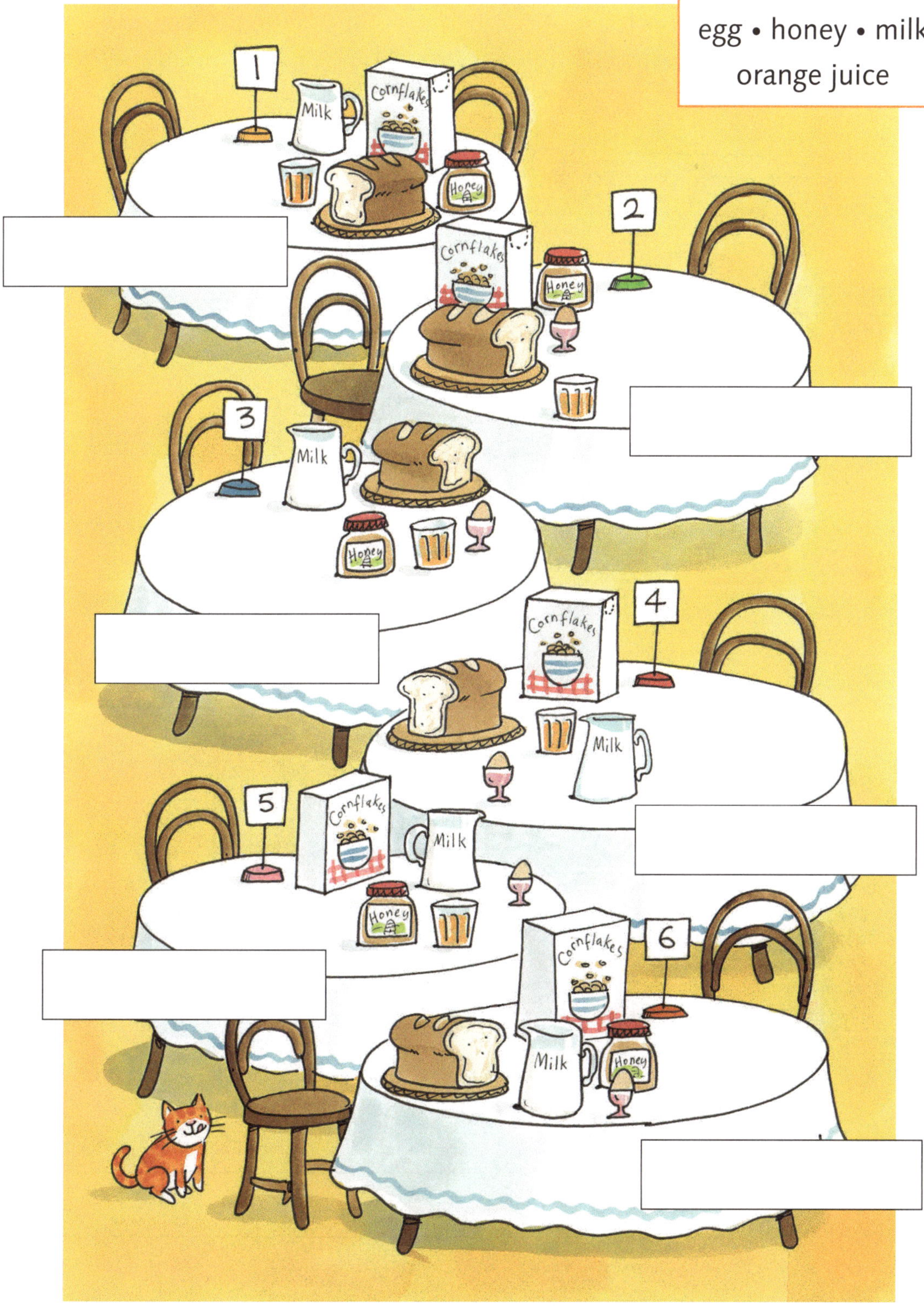

Über Lebensmittel sprechen, Frühstückswörter schreiben (S. 68)

Orange Island   In the storeroom

1 Listen. Write the shopping list.

CD 1.26

2 Write the sentences.

cornflakes

milk

eggs

bread

honey

orange juice

They need _____   _____

_____   _____

_____   _____

Einen Dialog verstehen, Bezeichnungen für Lebensmittel schreiben (S. 69 f.)

Orange Island   Fruit

I 🔤 **Complete the questions.**

> apple • banana
> grapefruit • lemon
> orange • strawberry

①

Can I have some
___ ___ ___ juice, please?

② Can I have some  _____ ,
_____ and
_____ juice, please?

③

_____
_____ and
_____ juice, please?

④ And you?

_____

_____

_____

Draw your fruit here.

Orange Island Food

1 Write the words.

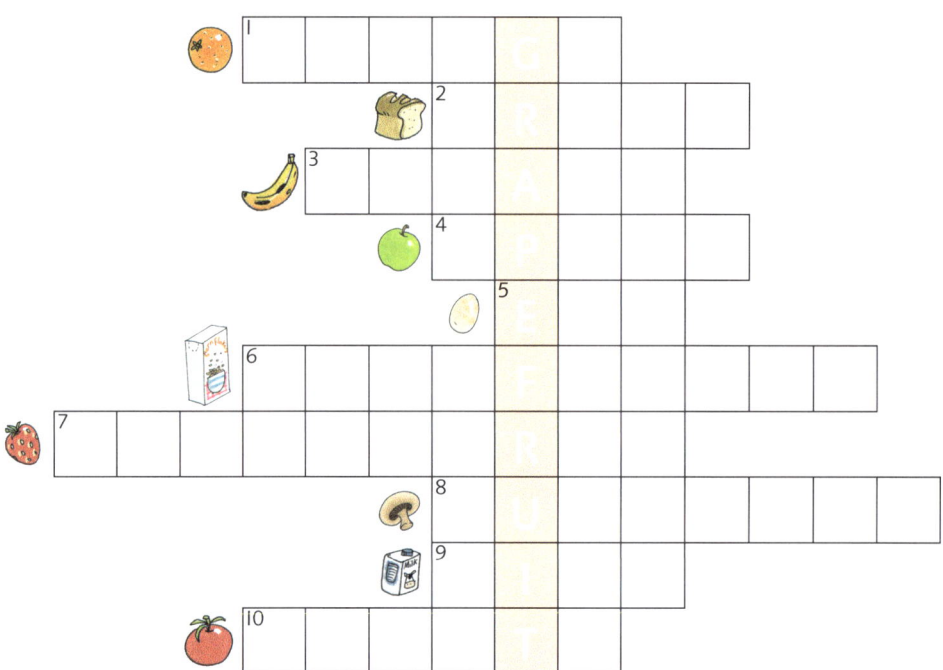

apple • banana • bread • breakfast • cheese • cornflakes
egg • fruit • green pepper • ham • honey • lemon • milk
mushroom • onion • orange • pizza • strawberry • tomato

2 Write what you like and what you don't like.

_____

_____

Ein Kreuzworträtsel lösen; schreiben, was man gern und nicht gern isst (S. 77 f.)

Orange Island   Ice cream

1 💬 **What ice cream have they got?**

🟡 vanilla   🟠 orange   🟢 apple   🔴 strawberry   ⚫ chocolate

Ginger ☐   Colin ☐   Penny ☐   Pablo ☐   Pepe ☐

2 ✏️ **Complete the sentences.**

Ginger has got _____ ice cream.

Colin has got _____

Penny _____

_____

_____

Sagen und schreiben, wer welches Eis hat (S. 80)

Orange Island Colin's fun food

1 💬 **What's your favourite fun food?**

tomato basket

grapefruit monster

2 💬 **What do you need for Colin's fun food?** *I need a tomato, an egg and cheese.*
Circle the food in the right colour.

(tomato basket)

(grapefruit monster)

(orange milkshake)

(banana split)

egg   bread   strawberry   grapefruit

vanilla ice cream   cheese

cornflakes

banana   tomato

chocolate ice cream

cookies   orange

milk   lemon

orange milkshake

banana split

Gerichte beschreiben, Bezeichnungen für Zutaten verstehen (S. 81 f.)

Portfolio: My fun food

Draw your fun food. Write what you need for your fun food.

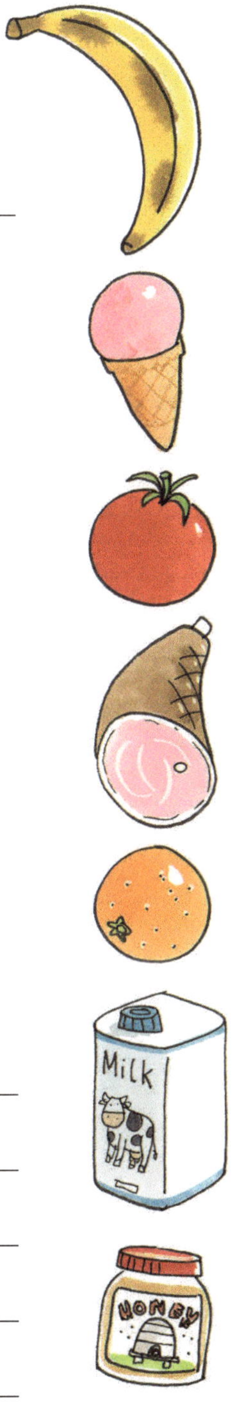

_____

(name of my fun food)

_____

_____

_____

_____

_____

Ein eigenes Gericht zeichnen und die verwendeten Zutaten aufschreiben (S. 82)

Orange Island   Was ich dazugelernt habe

1 ☐ Ich habe den *chant* „On Monday no cornflakes" aufgesagt.

2 ☐ Ich kann sagen, dass ich Hunger und Durst habe.

_____

3 ☐ Ich habe über Lebensmittel und Obst gesprochen. Schreibe so
viele Lebensmittel und Obstsorten auf, wie du kennst.

_____

_____

_____

_____

_____

4 ☐ Ich kann um etwas zu essen oder zu trinken bitten.

_____

5 ☐ Ich kann sagen, was ich gern und was ich nicht gern esse.

_____

_____

6 Ich habe diese Lieder gesungen:

☐ Oranges, tasty oranges

☐ Sandwiches

7 ☐ Ich kann sagen, welches mein Lieblingseis ist.

_____

8 ☐ Ich habe mir eine Speise ausgedacht und vorgestellt.

_____

Circus Island Mr Ringley's circus: the pictures

I 💬 Talk about the pictures. Cut out the pictures.

Bilder beschreiben und ausschneiden (S. 93)

Mr Ringley's circus: the story

I **Read the sentences. Glue the pictures in the right order.**

Mr Ringley was happy in his circus.

The clown said, 'Bye-bye, Mr Ringley.'

The elephant said, 'Bye-bye, Mr Ringley.'

The juggler said, 'Bye-bye, Mr Ringley.'

The horse said, 'Bye-bye, Mr Ringley.'

Mr Ringley put the message in a bottle.

Sätze lesen, Bilder in der richtigen Reihenfolge einkleben (S. 93)

Circus Island Animals

1 Write the words.

> bear
> elephant
> horse
> lion
> monkey
> parrot

elephant

bear

horse

2 What animals do they like?

> bears
> elephants
> horses
> lions
> parrots

I like _____

_____

_____

_____

_____

And you? _____

Tierwörter lesen und schreiben (S. 97 f.)

Circus Island Actions

I ✏️ **Write the words.**

> Clap your hands. • Close your
> eyes. • Jump up high. • Sing.
> Sit down. • Stamp your feet.
> Stand up. • Touch your toes.
> Turn around.

_____

_____

_____

_____

_____   _____

Anweisungen schreiben (S. 101)

Circus Island   A silly clown

1 ✏️ **Write the sentences.**

②

① _____

_____

_____

③ _____

_____

⑥ _____

_____

④ _____

_____

⑤ _____

_____

The clown can stand on his head. • The clown's hands are on his eyes.
The clown has got his toes in his mouth. • The clown's hair is green.
The clown's feet are on his nose. • The clown's arms are on his legs.

2 ✏️ **Draw a silly clown.**
Write about the clown.

_____

_____

_____

Sätze Bildern zuordnen (S. 104)

Portfolio: My circus act

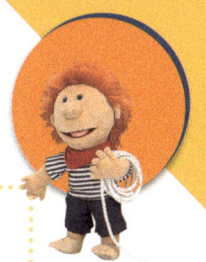

Write the name of your circus.

Draw or glue a picture of your circus act in the ring.

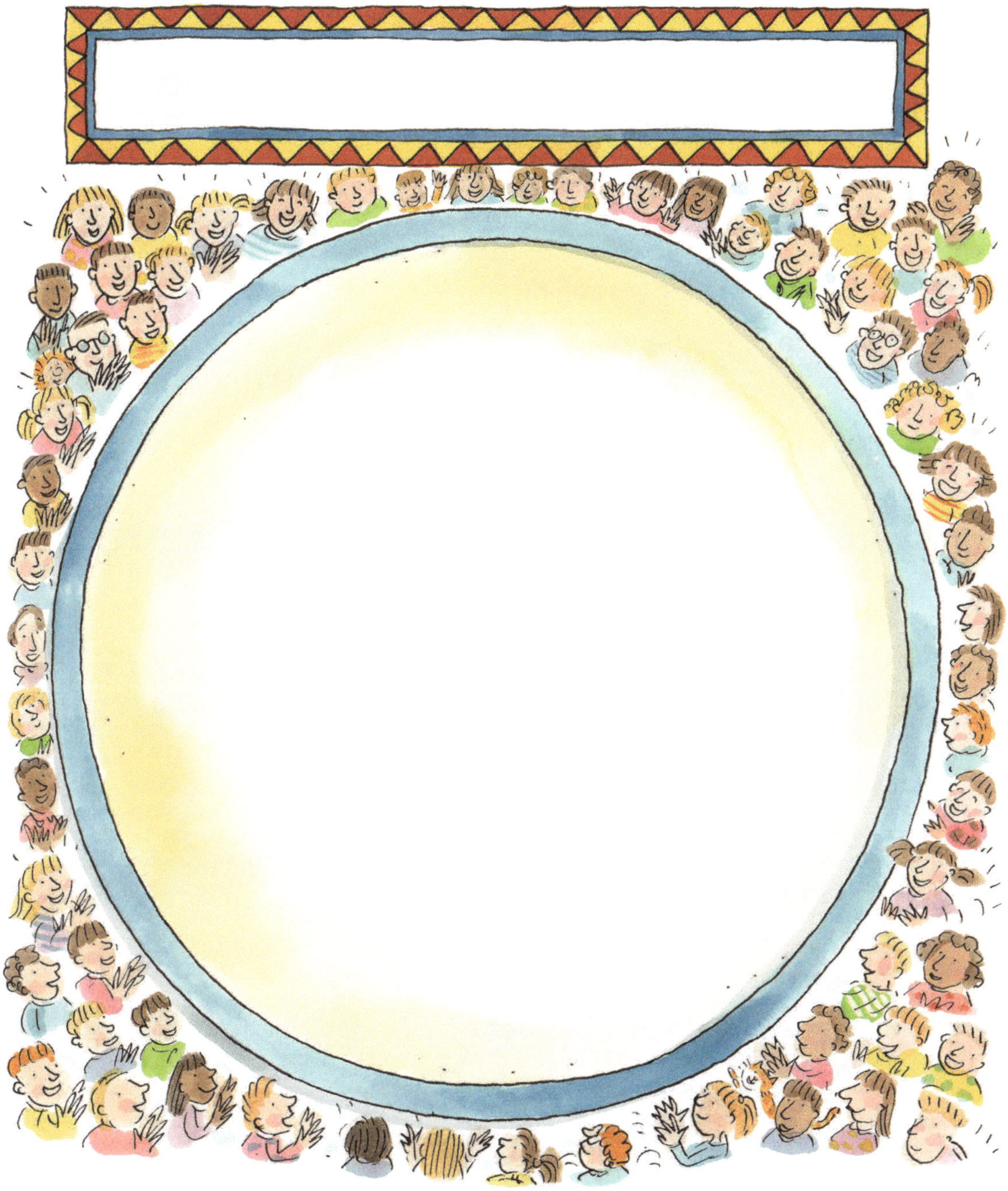

(name)

(act)

Circus Island Was ich dazugelernt habe

1 ☐ Ich habe die Geschichte „Mr Ringley's Circus" gehört.

2 ☐ Ich kenne die englischen Wörter für Tiere im Zirkus.
Schreibe sie auf.

_____

_____

3 ☐ Ich habe den *chant* „Five in the circus" aufgesagt.

4 Ich habe diese Lieder gesungen:
☐ Wake up in the morning
☐ Reach for the sky

5 ☐ Ich kann sagen, welches Tier ich mag.

_____

6 ☐ Ich kenne die englischen Wörter für Körperteile.
Schreibe die Körperteile auf.

_____

_____

7 ☐ Ich kann als Dompteur Anweisungen geben.
Schreibe die Anweisungen auf.

_____

_____

_____

_____

8 ☐ Ich habe folgenden *circus act* vorgeführt:

_____

_____

I Complete the speech bubbles.

cloudy • cold • foggy
rainy • snowy • sunny
warm • windy

What's the weather like today?

It's _____ and _____

1

What's the weather _____

2

_____ _____

What's _____ _____

3

_____

_____ _____

4

_____ _____

_____ _____

5

_____

Rainbow Island A walk around the island

1 Write the sentences.

2  Number the pictures. Read the new story.

Let's walk around the island.
It's such a sunny day.

Climb up and down the mountain.
Don't fall into the mud.
Now let's have our picnic.
Walk across the river.
Walk quickly through the grass.

_____

Swish, swash, swish.
Then hurry along the way.

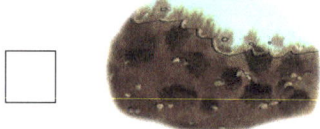

Let's walk around the island.
It's such a sunny day.

_____

Let's walk around the island.
It's such a sunny day.

Squelch, squelch, squelch.
Then hurry along the way.

_____

Huff, puff, huff.
Then hurry along the way.

Let's walk around the island.
It's such a sunny day.

_____

Let's walk around the island.
It's such a sunny day.

Splish, splash, splish.
Then hurry along the way.

_____

Munch, crunch, slurp.
Then hurry along the way.

Sätze in einer Geschichte ergänzen, eine Geschichte vorlesen (S. 124)

An island puzzle: the pictures

I   Cut out the pictures in the puzzle.

Bilder benennen und ausschneiden (S. 125)

Rainbow Island

An island puzzle: the words

I   Read the words. Glue the pictures on the right word.

	A	B	C	D
1	sunny	trees	butterfly	chameleon
2	mountain	trees	Ginger	Dr Heal
3	birds	trees	river	Dr Heal
4	cloudy	flowers	river	bird
5	rainy	flowers	mud	river

Wörter lesen und die Puzzlebilder einkleben (S. 125 f.)

Rainbow Island   I know these words

1 💭 **Number the pictures.**

2 ✏️ **Write the words. Check your spelling.**
   Look at your Pupil's Book word list on pages 37–39.

Nature	Weather	Animals

3 ✏️ **Can you add more words?**

© 2009 Cornelsen Verlag, Berlin · Alle Rechte vorbehalten.

Bilder in der richtigen Reihenfolge nummerieren, Wörter nach Wortfeldern ordnen (S. 127)

Portfolio: My photo

Draw your photo. Write what's in your photo.

There's grass and
a river. Dr Heal is on
the grass. There's
a butterfly on Dr Heal's toe.

_____

_____

_____

_____

Ein Bild malen und beschreiben (S. 128)

Rainbow Island Was ich dazugelernt habe

1 Ich habe diese Lieder gesungen:

☐ The weather song

☐ Race you down the mountain

2 ☐ Ich kann jemanden fragen, wie das Wetter heute ist.

_____

3 ☐ Ich kann sagen,
    wie das Wetter heute ist.

_____

_____

4 ☐ Ich kann die Natur beschreiben.
    Schreibe auf, was es in der Natur gibt.

_____

_____

_____

5 ☐ Ich habe die Geschichte „Ginger's Picnic" gehört.

6 Ich habe diese Reime aufgesagt:

☐ I like mud

☐ Don't pick flowers

7 ☐ Ich habe einen Rundgang über die Insel unternommen:
    A walk around the island.

8 ☐ Ich habe ein Bild von Rainbow Island gemalt und es vorgestellt.

Robot Island   Where's the mouse?

1 🖊 **Write the words.**

keyboard
mouse
notebook
window

2 🖊 **Where's the mouse?**

| behind • on • under | bed • chair • clock • table |

The mouse is

The mouse is

_____

_____

_____

_____

_____

_____

Computerwörter schreiben; aufschreiben, wo sich etwas befindet (S. 135 f.)

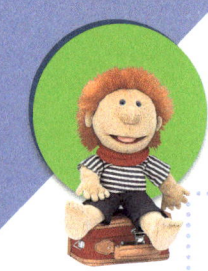

Robot Island Vehicles in the city

I Count the vehicles. Write how many vehicles there are.

bikes
buses
cars
motorbikes
planes
trains

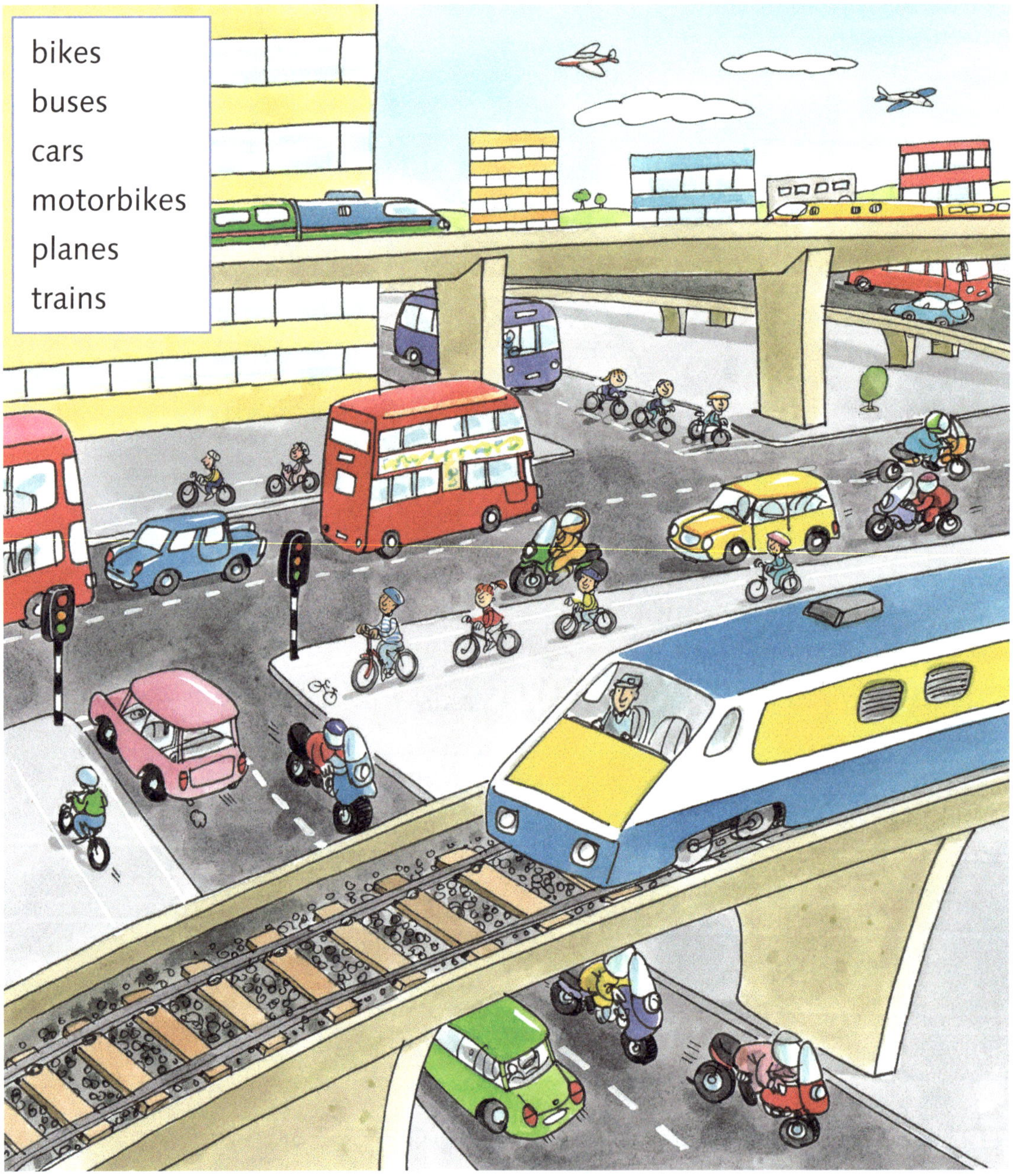

There are 4 buses. ______________________

______________________ ______________________

______________________ ______________________

Fahrzeuge zählen und die Anzahl aufschreiben (S. 138)

Robot Island   The way to Professor Bit's house

1 🔘 Listen and draw a line from the computer shop to
CD 2.28 Professor Bit's house.

2 ✏️ **Complete the sentences.**

| Go to |
| Turn left |
| Turn right |

1 _____ the red house.

2 _____ at the red house.

3 _____ the jeans shop.

4 _____ into Robot street.

5 _____ the green house. It's number II. It's my house.

Eine Wegbeschreibung verstehen, Satzteile ergänzen (S. 140)

Robot Island   Professor Bit's workshop

 I   **Listen. What's broken and what's fixed?**
CD 2.31   **Cross out the wrong word.**

> 1 The toaster is ~~fixed~~ / broken.
>
> 2 The radio is ~~fixed~~ / broken.
>
> 3 The Discman is fixed / ~~broken~~.
>
> 4 The notebook is ~~fixed~~ / broken.
>
> 5 The skateboard is fixed / ~~broken~~.

Einen Hörtext verstehen (S. 145)

Fruit / Pizza

Actions

Vehicles	House	Professor Bit can fix it
bike	bathroom	Discman
bus	bedroom	Game Boy
car	garden	notebook
motorbike	house	radio
plane	kitchen	robot
train	living room	skateboard

Clothes	Fairy tales	Personal words
cap	castle	
dress	fairy	
shirt	king	
shoes	prince	
shorts	queen	
socks	wolf	

School things

book
pencil
pencil case
rubber
schoolbag

Breakfast

bread
cornflakes
egg
honey
milk
orange juice

Fruit

apple
banana
grapefruit
lemon
orange
strawberry

Pizza

cheese
green pepper
ham
mushroom
onion
tomato

Animals

bear
elephant
horse
lion
monkey
parrot

Circus

animal trainer
circus
clown
juggler
ringmaster
tightrope walker

Actions

clap your hands
close your eyes
flap your arms
jump up high
reach for the sky
sing
sit down
stamp your feet
stand up
touch your nose
turn around
wiggle your fingers

Weather

cloudy
cold
rainy
sunny
warm
windy

Nature

bird
butterfly
flower
mountain
river
tree

Robot Island   Professor Bit's robot

1  Read the sentences. Number the sentences.

☐ Professor Bit's robot can walk.

☐ Professor Bit's robot can clean his desk.

☐ Professor Bit's robot can carry his bag.

☐ Professor Bit's robot can speak.

☐ Professor Bit's robot can open the window.

2 Write what your robot can do.

My robot can _____

_____

_____

_____

Sätze lesen und in der richtigen Reihenfolge nummerieren (S. 147 f.)

Robot Island   An e-mail to Professor Bit

I [ab] Write an e-mail to Professor Bit.

Dear Professor Bit, • … is/are great.
I like … • There's … • There are …
Thank you. • From, …

Thank you
To: professor.bit@cornelsen.de
Subject: Thank you

Eine E-Mail schreiben (S. 149 f.)

Portfolio: My dream house

Draw your dream house. Write about your dream house.

> There's … • There are … • I've got … in my …

_____

_____

_____

Sein Traumhaus malen (S. 144)

Robot Island   Was ich dazugelernt habe

1 ☐ Ich kenne die englischen Bezeichnungen von
Verkehrsmitteln.

_____

_____

2 Ich habe diese Lieder gesungen:
☐ Let's go
☐ My skateboard's broken

3 ☐ Ich kann einen Weg auf Englisch beschreiben.

⌐ _____   ⌐ _____   ↑ _____

4 ☐ Ich habe den *chant* „Robot in the bedroom"
aufgesagt.

5 ☐ Ich kann sagen, dass etwas kaputt ist.

_____

6 ☐ Ich habe folgenden Dialog gespielt: In a workshop.

7 ☐ Ich habe mein Traumhaus gemalt und vorgestellt.

8 ☐ Ich habe die Geschichte
„Professor Bit's robot" gehört.

Fantasy Island   A story for Ginger

I  Write the sentences.

The wolf is sad.

Hello, Father. Please come in.

The prince is in the castle.

The king, the queen and
the prince are happy.

Hello, Wolf. Please come in.

Sätze Bildern zuordnen (S. 156)

Fantasy Island When's your party?

1 Complete the speech bubbles.

> Monday • Tuesday
> Wednesday • Thursday
> Friday • Saturday • Sunday

1

> When's your party?

> My party is on Tuesday at 7 o'clock.

2

> When's _____ ?

> _____
> Friday ____ 5 _____ .

3

> _____
> _____

Saturday
party
6 O'clock

> _____
> _____

2 Write an invitation to your birthday party.
Look at Pupil's Book page 29.

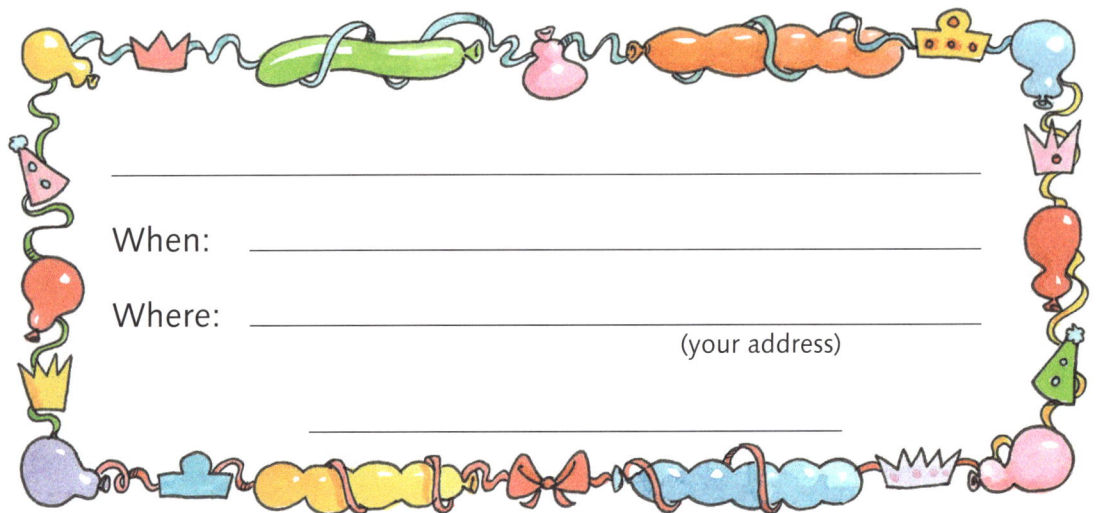

When: _____

Where: _____
(your address)

_____

Sätze vervollständigen, eine Geburtstagseinladung schreiben (S. 158)

Fantasy Island   An invitation to a party

I  Write the sentences.   2 🗨 Act out the scene.

> Can you come? • Goodbye. • Thank you.
> See you on Sunday. • Oh – a party.
> Here's an invitation from Prince Charming.
> Goodbye, Little Red Riding Hood.
> See you on Sunday. • Yes, I can. • Great.

(LRRH = Little Red Riding Hood)

Ravi: _____

LRRH: _____

_____ _____

_____ _____

_____ _____ _____ _____

_____ _____ _____

_____ _____

_____ _____

_____ _____

_____ _____

Sätze eines Dialogs in der richtigen Reihenfolge aufschreiben (S. 159 f.)

Fantasy Island   Clothes

1   Write the words.

cap
dress
jeans
pullover
shirt
shoes
shorts
socks
T-shirt

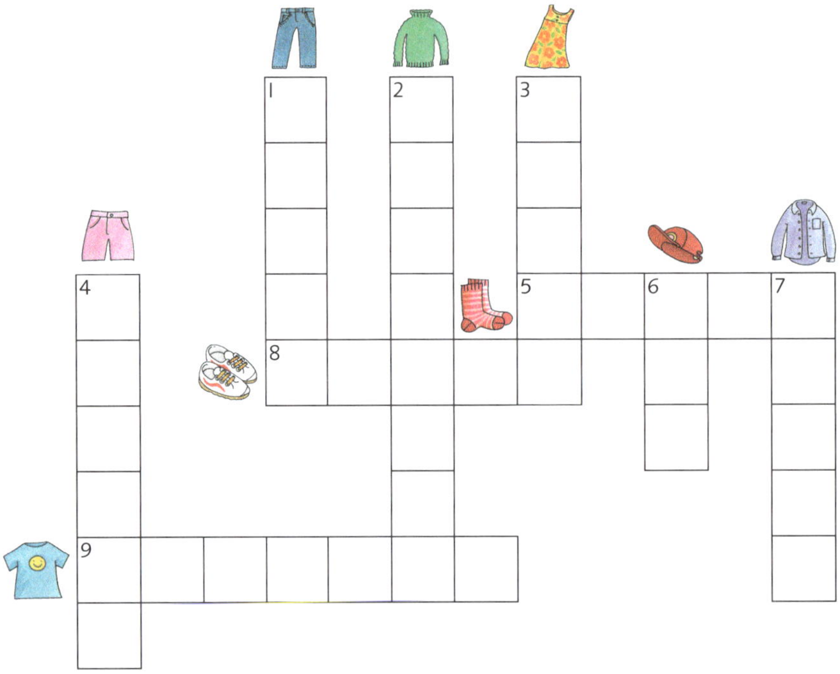

2   What are they wearing?

I'm Tom. I'm wearing a _____ .

It's red. My _____ are blue.

My _____ are orange.

My name is Sally.

_____

_____

_____

3   What are you wearing?

_____

_____

_____

Ein Kreuzworträtsel lösen, Sätze ergänzen, die eigene Kleidung beschreiben (S. 162)

Fantasy Island Cinderella

I   Cut out the pictures.

Bilder ausschneiden (S. 168)

What's your wish? Draw a picture. Write the words.

I want _____

_____

_____

_____

_____

_____

_____

Ein Bild malen und beschreiben (S. 164)

Fantasy Island   Was ich dazugelernt habe

1 ☐ Ich kann jemanden zu einer Party einladen.

_____

2 ☐ Ich kann sagen, wann eine Party stattfindet.

_____

3   Ich kenne diese Märchenfiguren auf Englisch:

_____

_____

_____

4   Ich habe diese Lieder gesungen:
   ☐ Skidamarink
   ☐ Pick it up
   ☐ For he's a jolly good fellow

5 ☐ Ich kann sagen, was ich gerade anhabe.

_____

6 ☐ Ich habe den Reim „I paint my fingernails" aufgesagt.

7 ☐ Ich kann sagen, was ich mir
     von einer Fee wünsche.

8 ☐ Ich habe ein Cinderella-Märchenbuch gebastelt.

Special days My birthday

1 When's your birthday?

1

arm   arm

2

arm   arm

| January |
| February |
| March |
| April |
| May |
| June |
| July |
| August |
| September |
| October |
| November |
| December |

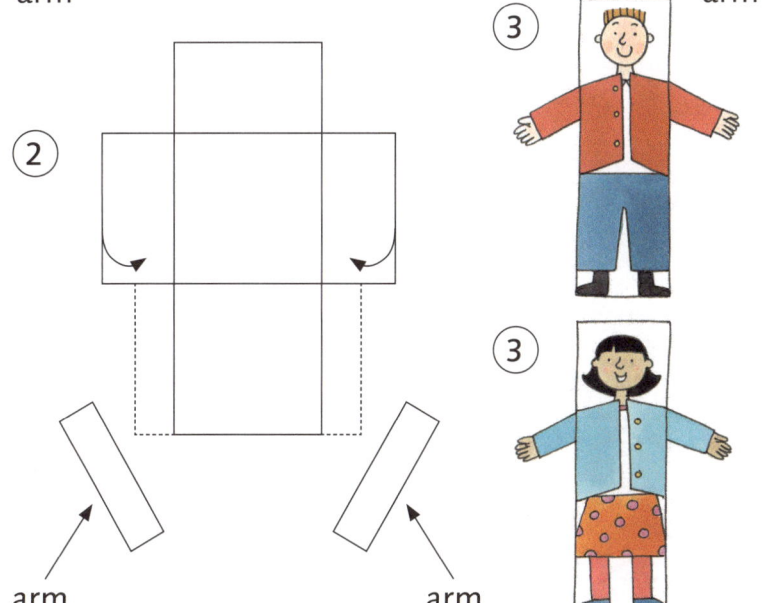

3   4 Tobi 16 May

3   4 Maria 28 November

Figuren für einen Geburtstagskalender basteln (S. 176)

Special days A Christmas card

I  Write a card.

a • and • Dear • From, Happy New Year. • Merry Christmas

Eine Grußkarte schreiben (S. 180)

Word fields

Breakfast

_____

_____

● _____

_____

_____

Fruit

_____

_ _ _ _ _ _ _ _ _ _ _

_____

● _ _ _ _ _ _ _ _ _ _

_____

_____

_____

Pizza

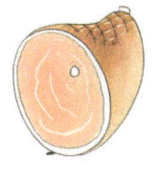

_____

_ _ _ _ _ _ _ _ _

_____

_____

_____

_____

Word fields

Animals

_____ _____

_____

_____ ____

_____

_____

_____

Weather

_____

_____

_____

_____

_____

_____

Nature

_____

_____

_____

_____

_____

_____

Word fields

Vehicles

 _____

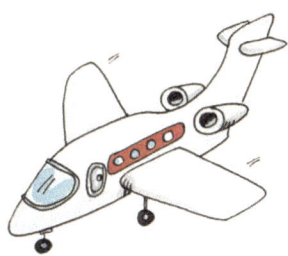

_____

_____

_____

 _____

_____

House

_____   _____

_____

_____

_____   _____

Clothes

_____   _____

_____

 _____

_____   _____

_____

Ginger Early Start Edition

Lehrwerk für den früh beginnenden Englischunterricht

Activity Book 3
Class 3

Erarbeitet von
Birgit Hollbrügge, Bielefeld; Ulrike Kraaz, Werther

Beratende Mitwirkung
Hans Bebermeier, Bielefeld; Ingrid Fechner, Kassel; Reingard Graupner, Hohenstein-Ernstthal;
Evelin Hartmann-Kleinschmidt, Delbrück; Dr. Sabine Herfurt, Berlin; Judith Kemper, Borken; Tamara Kipper,
Düsseldorf; Katrin Lehmann, Klein Wanzleben; Amke Lindenmann, Wedemark; Petra Ilona Sälzer, Kamen;
Britta Schmidt, Pasewalk; Kerstin Scholz, Thallwitz; Ursula Stoll, Hüllhorst; Birgit Waatsack, Langenhagen;
Hannelore Wuntke, Weimar

Verlagsredaktion
Marie Keenoy (Projektleitung), Elke Lehmann (verantwortlich), Dr. Eva Grabowski, Rebecca Kaplan
sowie Theresa Hoffmann (Assistenz)

Illustration
Jan Lewis, Pangbourne, England

Umschlaggestaltung
Anna Bakalovic für Buchgestaltung+, Berlin

Layoutkonzept
Susanne Meyer

Technische Umsetzung
Kati Klaeske, Berlin

Bildquellen
Eising FoodPhotography, München (S. 14); Lox und Bergmann, Fotodesign, Berlin (Fotos von Ginger)

Zusatzmaterial zum Activity Book
Lernsoftware Ginger *My first English Coach*, ISBN 978-3-464-35673-9

www.cornelsen.de

1. Auflage, 12. Druck 2022

© 2009 Cornelsen Verlag, Berlin
© 2017 Cornelsen Verlag GmbH, Berlin

Druck: Livonia Print, Riga

ISBN 978-3-06-031350-1

PEFC zertifiziert
Dieses Produkt stammt aus nachhaltig
bewirtschafteten Wäldern und kontrollierten
Quellen.

www.pefc.de

PEFC/12-31-006